count and see

by tana hoban

MACMILLAN PUBLISHING CO., INC.

NEW YORK

6 7 8 9 10

The photographs in this book were taken with the Beseler Topcon RE Super D (35mm) camera, using 58mm, 80mm and 135mm lenses. The films used were Plus-X Pan and Tri-X, developed in Ethol UFG and printed on Varigam paper with Dektol developer.

1
ONE

2
TWO

3

THREE

FOUR

5

FIVE

6

SIX

SEVEN

8

EIGHT

NINE

10
TEN

11
ELEVEN

12

TWELVE

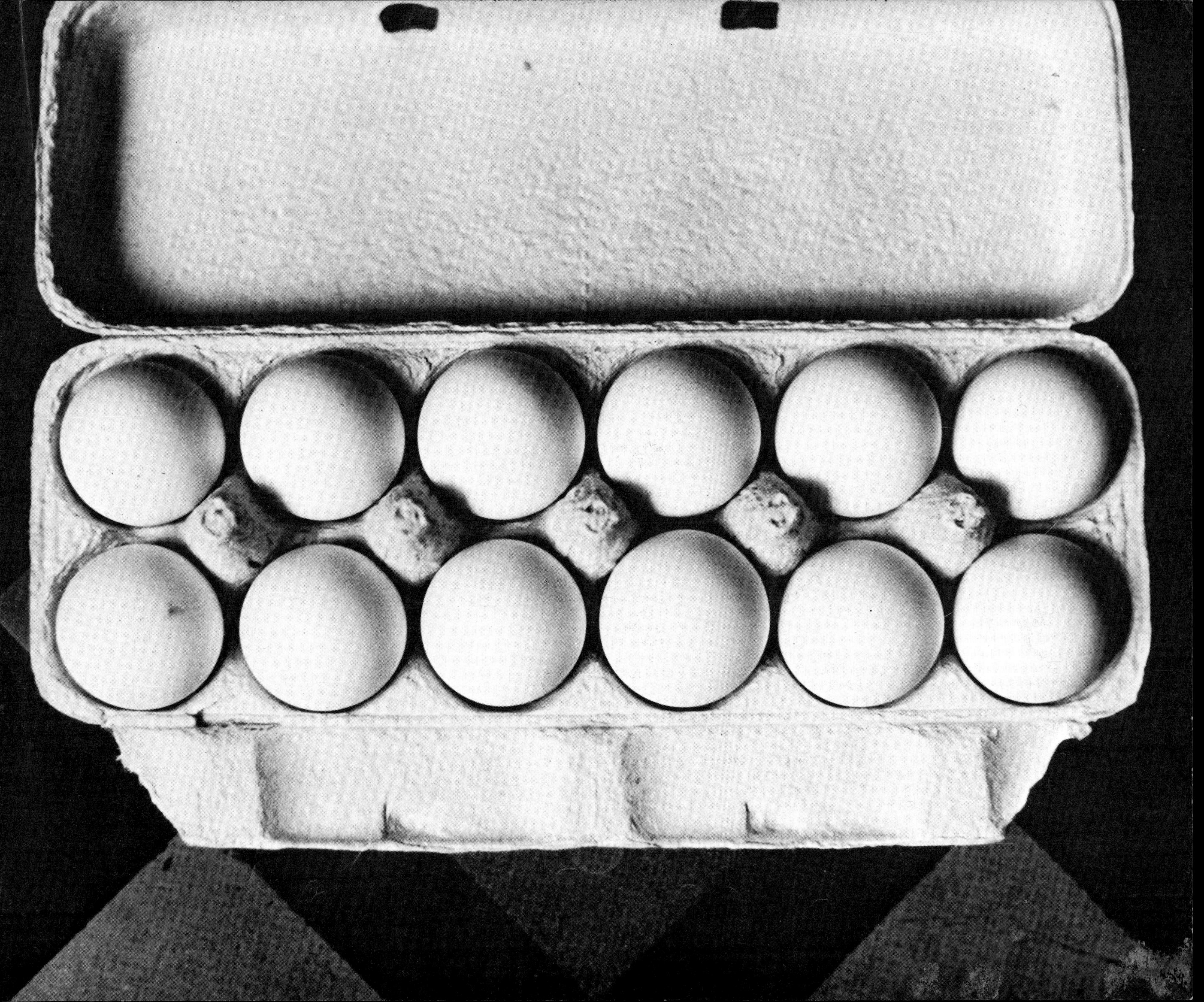

13

THIRTEEN

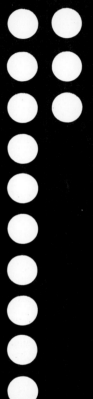

14

FOURTEEN

15

FIFTEEN

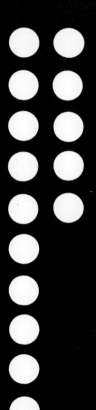

20
TWENTY

30
THIRTY

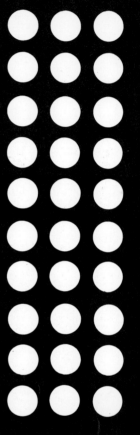

40

FORTY

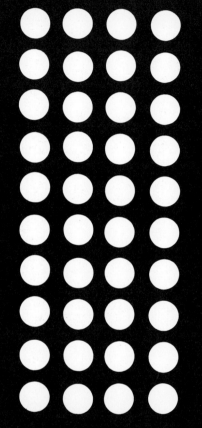

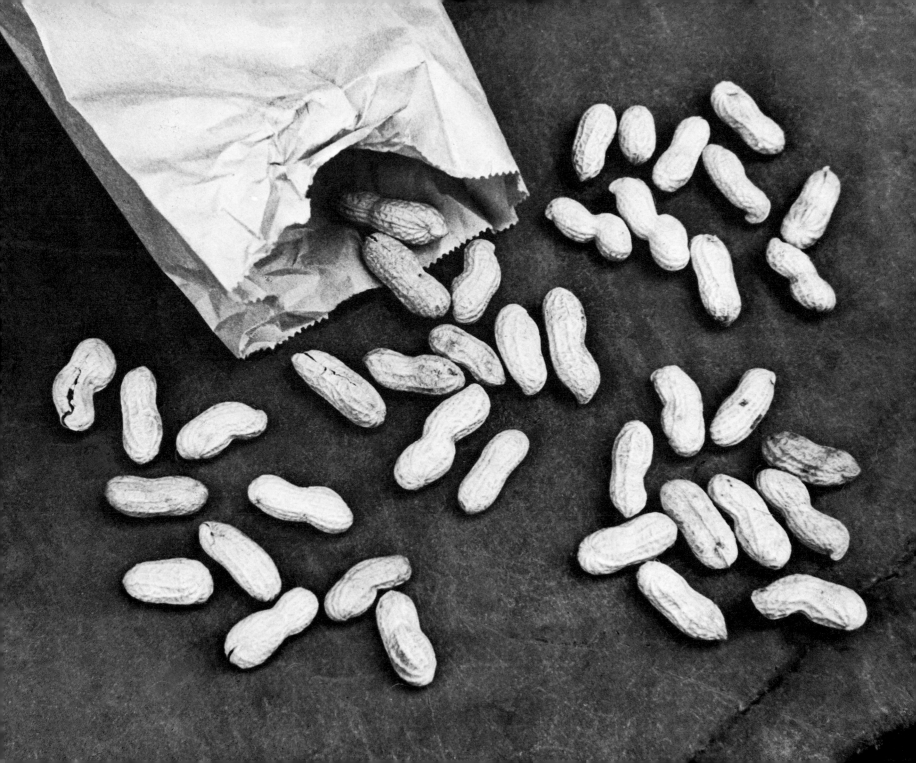

50
FIFTY

100

ONE HUNDRED